RAND NATIONAL DEFENSE RESEARCH INSTITUTE

A Program Manager's Guide for Program Improvement in Ongoing Psychological Health and Traumatic Brain Injury Programs

The RAND Toolkit, Volume 4

Gery W. Ryan, Carrie M. Farmer, David M. Adamson, Robin M. Weinick

Prepared for the Office of the Secretary of Defense and the Defense Centers of Excellence
for Psychological Health and Traumatic Brain Injury

This research was sponsored by the the Office of the Secretary of Defense (OSD) and the Defense Centers of Excellence for Psychological Health and Traumatic Brain Injury. It was conducted in the Forces and Resources Policy Center, a RAND National Defense Research Institute (NDRI) program. NDRI is a federally funded research and development center sponsored by the OSD, the Joint Staff, the Unified Combatant Commands, the Navy, the Marine Corps, the defense agencies, and the defense Intelligence Community under Contract W74V8H-06-C-0002.

Library of Congress Cataloging-in-Publication Data is available for this publication.

ISBN: 978-0-8330-8052-3

The RAND Corporation is a nonprofit institution that helps improve policy and decisionmaking through research and analysis. RAND's publications do not necessarily reflect the opinions of its research clients and sponsors.

Support RAND—make a tax-deductible charitable contribution at www.rand.org/giving/contribute.html

RAND® is a registered trademark.

RAND OFFICES
SANTA MONICA, CA • WASHINGTON, DC
PITTSBURGH, PA • NEW ORLEANS, LA • JACKSON, MS • BOSTON, MA
DOHA, QA • CAMBRIDGE, UK • BRUSSELS, BE
www.rand.org

Preface

Between 2001 and 2011, the U.S. Department of Defense (DoD) has implemented numerous programs to support service members and their families in coping with the stressors from a decade of the longstanding conflicts in Iraq and Afghanistan. These programs, which address both psychological health and traumatic brain injury (TBI), number in the hundreds and vary in their size, scope, and target population. To ensure that resources are wisely invested and maximize the benefits of such programs, the Assistant Secretary of Defense for Health Affairs asked the RAND National Defense Research Institute to develop a set of tools to assist with understanding, evaluating, and improving program performance.

With funding from the Defense Centers of Excellence for Psychological Health and Traumatic Brain Injury (DCoE), RAND developed a toolkit consisting of four tools:

- The **RAND Program Classification Tool** allows decisionmakers to characterize and compare programs along a number of dimensions, including whether the programs have specified goals, the clinical and nonclinical areas that the programs address, and whether an evaluation has been conducted (Volume 1).
- The **RAND Online Measure Repository** offers support in identifying appropriate outcome metrics for assessing program performance against specified goals and for conducting formal program outcome evaluations (Volume 2).
- The **RAND Program Expansion Tool** offers support in assessing existing evidence regarding the effectiveness of an individual program and determining whether the evidence justifies continuing or expanding the program (Volume 3).
- The **RAND Program Manager's Guide** helps managers assess program performance, consider options for improvement, implement solutions, then assess whether the changes worked (Volume 4).

This report describes the fourth of these tools, the RAND Program Manager's Guide for Program Improvement. This guide is intended to help those responsible for managing or implementing programs to conduct assessments of how well the program is performing and implement solutions for improving performance. Specifically, the tool is intended to provide practical guidance in program improvement and continuous quality improvement for all programs. As this guide is written as a common-sense approach to program assessment and improvement, we note that it does not describe formal evaluation methods. Many resources are available to support such efforts; e.g., DCoE "Program Evaluation Guide" (2012).

This report is likely to be of interest to individuals who are responsible for managing or implementing programs that provide care to service members experiencing mental health problems or TBI, as well as staff working to improve program performance.

This research was sponsored sponsored by the Office of the Secretary of Defense and DCoE and conducted within the Forces and Resources Policy Center of the RAND National Defense Research Institute, a federally funded research and development center sponsored by the Office of the Secretary of Defense, the Joint Staff, the Unified Combatant Commands, the Navy, the Marine Corps, the defense agencies, and the defense Intelligence Community.

For more information on the RAND Forces and Resources Policy Center, see http://www.rand.org/nsrd/ndri/centers/frp.html or contact the director (contact information is provided on the web page).

Contents

Figures and Tables

Tables

Summary

To meet the growing need for services to support psychological health and care for traumatic brain injury (TBI), the Department of Defense (DoD) has developed and implemented a wide range of programs in recent years (Weinick et al., 2011). Given limited resources and the considerable investments that have been made in developing these programs, it is critical to ensure that programs are operating as effectively and efficiently as possible. To do this, program performance must be assessed on a regular basis and programs must continuously seek to optimize and improve performance. Without knowing the areas where a program may be falling short, it is not possible to ensure that the program is delivering the best possible services and operating as effectively and efficiently as possible.

This report describes a tool intended as a guide for program managers and others who seek to assess the performance of ongoing programs and improve their quality. In presenting this tool, we are mindful of the realities of program improvement and assessment activities in military settings. Because of military command structures, decisions about the need to conduct program improvement activities may not reside with the individual who created the program or the individual charged with managing it. Furthermore, individuals responsible for managing the program may not necessarily control how the program is implemented. Because of these realities, we adopted an approach to program improvement in this guide that can be implemented by individuals with varying degrees of control over the program that they manage. In addition, since there is wide variation in the types of psychological health and TBI programs conducted and/or funded by DoD, we chose to keep the tool focused generally on program improvement rather than attempting to address specific elements of the DoD programs in this area. We felt that this general approach would be more useful to the range of potential users, who can then adapt this approach to program-specific conditions.

The tool is organized around a series of key questions about program improvement in general. The questions can be adapted to specific DoD psychological health or TBI programs as needed.

The tool's key questions include the following:

- **Is the program accomplishing its intended goals?** The first step in assessing program performance is to determine whether the program is working well. This step involves identifying whether the program has clearly defined goals, articulating those goals as clearly as possible (or defining them if none can be identified), and determining how best to measure the program's performance in reaching its goals.
- **If the program is not accomplishing its intended goals, where are problems arising?** If the program is not working as well as expected, the next step is to pinpoint as specifi-

cally as possible what is wrong. Often, this step involves describing clearly how the program is supposed to work, identifying the key program positions and the players who fill them, and tracing the activities of these key players across the program's operations.

- **What are potential solutions for addressing the problems and what can guide the selection of which ones to implement?** Once the problems have been pinpointed, a range of potential solutions can be identified and considered according to their feasibility and their likelihood of addressing the problem. Potential solutions can come from many different sources. They are found in the professional literature, suggested by people who may be interviewed, or derived from common sense and past experiences. The source of the solutions is less relevant; what is important is considering as wide and as comprehensive a range of potential solutions as possible, regardless of whether they seem feasible when first considered. Selecting which solutions to implement involves rating the proposed solutions by potential effectiveness, cost, and feasibility, and then determining the best solution through discussions with team members and other stakeholders.
- **How can solutions be implemented?** Implementing a solution or set of solutions typically involves multiple steps, such as developing an implementation plan, informing people about coming changes, ensuring that people understand why the changes are needed, and making people in the chain of command aware of the implementation plan. In addition, implementing most changes means that at least some people will need to change how they think and what they do.
- **How well are the solutions as implemented addressing the problem?** Because many programs may have limited available time or resources, the most practical method for assessing whether the changes have improved program performance is to follow a relatively simple approach known as "Plan—Do—Study—Act." This approach could also be known as "try it and see if it works."
- **How can a program be monitored to ensure continued success?** Once the specific problems identified have been addressed and the program is performing at its expected level, it is important to continue monitoring performance to ensure that the program remains free of those problems and to seek opportunities for further improvement. With periodic checks and ongoing monitoring, it is possible to identify early warning signs that program performance may be declining.

It is important to note that this report provides a tool to assess the performance of individual programs and is not intended for comparisons across programs to determine their relative effectiveness. In addition, this report does not provide the information necessary to determine whether a particular program should be ended, or whether additional resources should be devoted to improve the program's performance. Rather, this report enables program managers and others to assess whether the program is meeting its goals and, if not, to develop a plan for identifying and solving problems that are hampering performance.

Acknowledgments

We gratefully acknowledge the assistance of Anna Smith for the administrative support she provided preparing this document. In addition, we thank our project monitor at the Defense Centers of Excellence for Psychological Health and Traumatic Brain Injury, Mr. Yonatan Tyberg, as well as CAPT John Golden, COL (Ret) Charles Engel, Col Christopher Robinson, and CPT Dayami Liebenguth, for their support of our work. We also appreciate the valuable insights we received from Ian Coulter and Laurie Martin.

Abbreviations

CQI	continuous quality improvement
DCoE	Defense Centers of Excellence for Psychological Health and Traumatic Brain Injury
DoD	Department of Defense
RCT	randomized controlled trial
SMART	Specific, Measurable, Attainable, Relevant, and Time-Bound
TBI	traumatic brain injury

CHAPTER ONE

Introduction

Context

Between 2001 and mid-2011, more than 2.3 million service members were deployed in support of military operations in Iraq and Afghanistan, including Operation Iraqi Freedom, Operation Enduring Freedom, and the recent operations in Iraq, Operation New Dawn. These operations were marked by multiple long deployments; nearly half of service members who deployed did so more than once during this time frame, with many serving in theater several times. Evidence suggests that a substantial number of service members have experienced combat and operational stress-related problems, such as posttraumatic stress disorder and depression, and others have been faced with ongoing problems as a result of traumatic brain injury (TBI) (Tanielian and Jaycox, 2008). Family members such as spouses and children of deployed service members have also experienced psychological health concerns as a consequence of the ongoing stress of these deployments.

To address these issues, numerous programs and activities related to psychological health and TBI have proliferated across the Department of Defense (DoD). At the request of DoD, RAND recently completed a systematic assessment to identify and catalog these programs, finding over 200 DoD programs addressing psychological health or TBI (Weinick et al., 2011). As these programs represent significant DoD investment, it is important to ensure a reasonable return on this investment by determining how well these programs are working and improving those that are underperforming. However, most programs are operating without a clear understanding of whether they are having their intended effect—to improve the psychological health and well-being of service members and their families—or any effect at all. Given this, DoD asked RAND's project team to create a practical guide that program managers might use to assess and improve program performance based on lessons learned from the earlier project and from our expertise in program assessment.

Purpose

There are numerous textbooks and documents that describe formal program evaluation, and this guide is not designed to duplicate their contents. Rather, it focuses on how ongoing programs might conduct improvement efforts. We believe that creating such a guide, based on the distilled experience and expertise of our evaluation team, represents an important contribution to the literature on program assessment and evaluation. More importantly, it should provide useful, practical guidance to DoD program managers and other decisionmakers faced with the need to assess and improve ongoing programs.

Figure 1.1 illustrates steps in the process of assessing and improving program performance. These steps correspond to the structure of this report. The first step is to determine whether the program is performing at the expected level. If it is not, the next steps are to determine what is wrong, identify the range of potential solutions, and choose the best solution for improving performance. The last step is to implement a process to monitor program performance on a regular basis, to ensure the program is operating optimally.

This report is intended as a common-sense approach to assessing and improving program performance. It is not meant to be used to conduct cross-program comparisons or to determine whether a particular program should be ended, or whether additional resources should be devoted to improve the program's performance; such information is available in Martin et al. (2014). We further note that this report should not be considered a program evaluation guide. Rather, this report enables program managers and others to assess whether a program is meeting its goals and, if not, to develop a plan for identifying and solving problems that are affecting performance.

Assessing Program Performance as Continuous Quality Improvement

It is important to note up front that assessing program performance should not be a one-time activity. Rather, it should be part of an ongoing effort by programs to operate as effectively and efficiently as possible. We conceptualize this process as continuous quality improvement, or CQI, a concept that has been adopted from the manufacturing industry (Deming, 1986) and applied to a range of settings, notably health care (Berwick, Godfrey, and Roessner, 1990;

Figure 1.1
Steps to Assess and Improve Program Performance

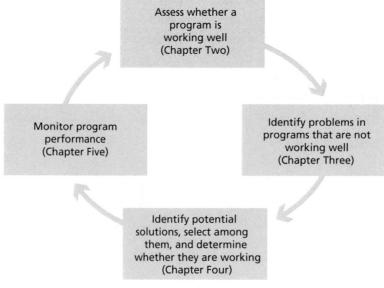

Shortell et al., 1995; Chowanec, 1994; Leebov and Ersoz, 2003; Solberg et al., 2001). CQI is a multistep approach designed to help programs and systems improve over time.

The general steps of CQI include

- making explicit the program's goals (i.e., what is it that the program hopes to provide to those people receiving services?)
- identifying one or more measures that will indicate how well the program is doing
- collecting the data to measure the program's performance
- evaluating the data to see to what degree the program's performance is meeting its goals
- determining how the program's performance might be improved
- implementing changes.

This cycle is repeated regularly by continuously collecting and analyzing performance data and making necessary changes to the program to ensure the program is meeting its goals. This report is designed to make this process explicit for program managers.

Who Should Read this Report?

This report will be useful for a number of audiences, and will be of interest primarily to those who direct or manage programs and are interested in understanding how to assess, monitor, and improve program performance. This report should also be useful to those who manage a portfolio of programs, as the process of monitoring and improving program performance is one that can and should be implemented across multiple programs. Finally, this report could also be useful for those who make decisions about program funding because it can serve as a starting point for determining how to direct additional resources to improve program performance, especially in the case where a sizable investment has already been made to implement a program. A related RAND report (Martin et al., 2014) addresses the issue of deciding whether to expand programs and how to assess the strength of the evidence available to support such a decision.

In presenting this tool, we are mindful of the realities of program improvement and assessment activities in military settings. Because of military command structures, decisions about the need to conduct program improvement activities may not reside with the individual who created the program or the individual charged with managing it. Furthermore, individuals responsible for managing the program may not necessarily control how the program is implemented. Because of these realities, we adopted an approach to program improvement in this guide that can be implemented by individuals with varying degrees of control over the program that they manage. In addition, since there is wide variation in the types of psychological health and TBI programs conducted and/or funded by DoD, we chose to keep the tool focused generally on program improvement rather than attempting to address specific elements of the DoD programs in this area. We felt this general approach would be more useful to the range of potential users, who can then adapt this approach to program-specific conditions.

Organization of This Report

The remainder of this report focuses on describing the CQI process in more detail, as it applies to programs. Chapter Two describes the steps needed to make program goals explicit, identify measures for assessing performance, and evaluate the data to determine whether a program is working as well as expected. The two chapters after that focus on identifying ways to improve program performance: Chapter Three describes how to identify potential problems that are affecting performance; Chapter Four details how to identify potential solutions to the problems, how to choose from among them, how to implement the chosen solution, and how to determine whether the solution is having the desired effect. Chapter Five discusses ongoing monitoring of programs and presents the report's conclusions.

Assessing Whether a Program Is Working Well

This chapter describes a process for assessing program performance. Its purpose is to describe an informal and exploratory approach that is intended to help administrators or managers of ongoing programs come to a clearer understanding of how well the program is working.

To know whether a program is working well, it is essential to assess the degree to which the program is reaching its overall goals and objectives for the specific population targeted and the degree to which each of the program's activities is being carried out so that it accomplishes its intended purpose.

As shown in Figure 2.1, this chapter addresses four questions intended to help program administrators undertake a program assessment:

- What is the program trying to accomplish?
- What parts of program performance require measurement?
- How should performance be measured?

Figure 2.1
Overview of Chapter Two

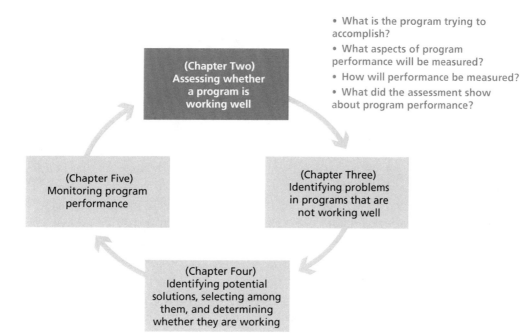

- What did the assessment show about program performance?

What Is the Program Trying to Accomplish?

To understand how well a program is working, a program manager first needs to specify what the program is intended to achieve. Who is the target population the program is designed to serve? What are the specific activities the program conducts? What are the expected outcomes from each activity? While the answers to these questions may be obvious in some cases, many programs may not have clearly articulated answers.

A first step is to address the following questions as specifically as possible:

- Who is included in the target population? Is there more than one target population (e.g., service members and family members)? How large is the target population?
- What is the overall purpose of the program? What need is it trying to fulfill?
- What are the components of the program, such as specific steps, activities, or processes?
- What are the specific goals or objectives of the program? What are the objectives of each of the steps, activities, or processes?
- What are the changes expected in the target population if the program accomplishes its goals?

The answers to these questions may depend on the program's stage of development. Programs that have been started only recently or are early in their development may not yet be delivering all intended services, conducting all activities, or reaching all targeted populations. Alternatively, well-established programs may have plans in the near future to change or expand in some way.

Throughout this report, we use a hypothetical program to illustrate the concepts we present (see "Hypothetical Program Example").

Hypothetical Program Example: ProgramX

ProgramX is a suicide prevention program for soldiers and their families that conducts two types of activities. The first is a briefing for all soldiers on suicide awareness. This briefing is intended to be delivered to all soldiers within two weeks of redeployment. The second is a hotline number for soldiers and their families to call if they or someone they know is in distress. The hotline is staffed 24 hours a day, seven days a week, and hotline staff are trained to respond to emergencies and refer callers for follow-up care.

While the ultimate goal of this program is to reduce the number of suicide attempts by soldiers, the program also intends to increase awareness about suicide and provide referrals to treatment for those in distress.

Specifying Program Goals the SMART Way

When specifying program goals, it is important to be as explicit as possible. One well-established way to do this is to develop goals that are SMART: Specific, Measurable, Attainable, Relevant, and Time-bound (Centers for Disease Control and Prevention, 2009; Doran, 1981).

Specific goals are those that are clear and convey to program staff and others the "who, what, when, where, and how" of the program. To do this, goals should mention the target population, the objectives, and the expected effects on the target population if the objectives are met (Acosta et al., 2014). For the suicide prevention program in our hypothetical example, one specific goal statement might be: "The goal of this program is to increase awareness about suicide [objective] among soldiers and their families [target population] so that more soldiers know where and how to get help [expected effect]."

Measurable goals are those that can be quantified. It is important to be clear about the size of the expected effect. In this example, measurable goals might be that 50 percent of soldiers will demonstrate an increased awareness of suicide warning signs and how to respond to them, that ten distressed individuals per month will be connected with appropriate care as a result of the program, or that the program will result in three fewer documented suicide attempts per year.

Estimating the size of the program's expected effect can be difficult. Program managers might consider a few sources of information to help with this. First, if the program draws from an evidence-based intervention, information from published literature about the intervention can inform expectations. For example, the hotline staff in the suicide prevention program example may use motivational interviewing to encourage soldiers with suicidal thoughts to seek follow-up care. Motivational interviewing is an evidence-based intervention for which clinical trials have demonstrated efficacy in various populations. Reviewing the literature about motivational interviewing can help determine the size of the effect that these clinical trials have demonstrated (e.g., the average change in the likelihood of seeking follow-up care) in the populations studied. This can be used to estimate the expected impact of the intervention on the program's target population.

Second, a program manager could look at the reported effectiveness of similar programs. For the suicide prevention program, it is likely that other programs using briefings or hotlines have been evaluated. Reviewing published reports describing the results of such evaluations can help determine the probable effect of a particular program.

Attainable goals are those that are realistic. In the suicide prevention example, it is probably not realistic to expect that the program will drop the suicide rate to zero. However, it may be realistic to expect that the program will result in two or three fewer documented suicide attempts per year.

Relevant goals are those that matter. An assessment of program performance will need to consider what is important to the various stakeholders in the program, such as the command and the program participants. In the example program, stakeholders might suggest that relevant goals would include reduction in the number of suicide attempts and increased awareness about suicide.

Time-bound goals are those that refer to meeting objectives within a specific time frame. For example, the suicide prevention program may specify that briefings to soldiers are provided *within two weeks* of redeployment, calls to the hotline are answered *in two rings or less*, or referrals to care are completed *within seven days*.

Using the SMART approach, a complete goal statement for the briefing component of the example suicide prevention program might be: "The goal of this program is to provide briefings within two weeks of redeployment [attainable, time-bound] that increase awareness about suicide [specific, relevant, measureable] among soldiers and their families [specific] so that more soldiers know where and how to get help [relevant because the expected effect is described]."

How to Decide What and How to Assess

After clarifying how the program is intended to work and specifying its goals, program managers (or whoever is assessing the program's performance) should determine what aspects of the program to assess and how to assess them. There are many different ways of assessing program performance.

What to Assess

Both processes and outcomes are important components of a program's success. Whether the assessment focuses on processes or outcomes depends on what type of question the assessment is asking: Has the program been implemented correctly (processes), or is the program making a difference to participants (outcomes), or both?

If the focus is on understanding how the mechanics of the program are working, program managers in the suicide prevention program example may want to know answers to the following process questions: What proportion of soldiers receives the briefing within two weeks of redeployment? Within four weeks? Do soldiers and their families know about the hotline? How many calls per day does the hotline receive? What is the nature of the calls (e.g., seeking a referral, needing emergency action, requesting information)? Who is making the calls (e.g., soldiers or their family members)?

If the program manager is interested in understanding whether the program has an effect on outcomes, it might be best to ask the following outcome questions: Are the targeted populations (e.g., soldiers and families) more aware of suicide risk factors? Has the number of documented suicide attempts or completed suicides changed? Have those who needed or requested referrals to mental health care received them? Have those with referrals pursued and received mental health care?

How to Assess

After determining whether to assess program processes, outcomes, or both, the next step is to specify how to assess whether the program is meeting its goals.

To start, it may be useful to diagram program activities and possible measures of them to understand what questions to ask about each piece. For example, referring again to the suicide prevention program, Figure 2.2 describes the suicide prevention briefing component of the program and Figure 2.3 describes the suicide hotline component of the program.

These figures illustrate the activities involved in the program as well as possible measures that could be used to understand how well each of the activities is working. For example, to understand the extent to which soldiers and their families know about the hotline (activity one), it would be important to measure the number or proportion of soldiers and family members who have heard of it.

Figure 2.2
Suicide Prevention Briefing Flow Diagram

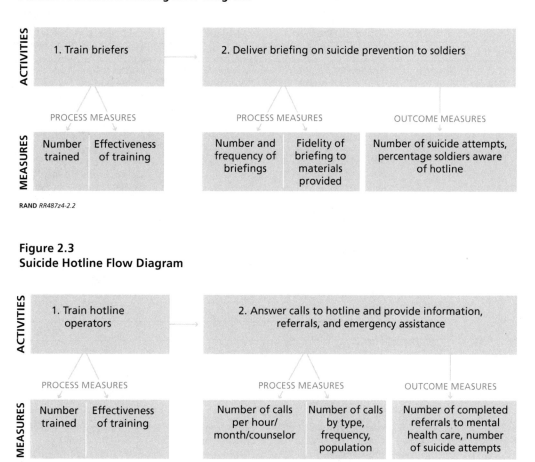

RAND *RR487z4-2.2*

Figure 2.3
Suicide Hotline Flow Diagram

RAND *RR487z4-2.3*

It is important to note that for this program, the two components (the briefing and the hotline) are interactive. The briefing in Figure 2.2 provides information to soldiers about the hotline, which then influences the first activity shown in Figure 2.3. Depending on the complexity of the program, it may be necessary to draw multiple flow diagrams. The process of mapping out the steps and components of a program, along with measures or questions, can help in determining what can or should be measured to assess program performance.

Once the activities and ways to measure each step are mapped out, the next task is to create a matrix of information on the program's activities or processes, the target populations, the intended goals, the measures used to determine whether the goals are being achieved, and a space to compare the goals with the actual results from the assessment. Table 2.1 illustrates a completed matrix for the suicide prevention program example above. Appendix A contains this matrix as a worksheet for program managers to use in assessing the performance of their programs.

Table 2.1
Matrix for Program Performance Assessment

Activity/Process	Target Population	Objective (Outcome/Process)	Measure	Goal	Results
Briefing on suicide					
Step 1: Train Briefers	Briefers	**Process:** Effectively train an adequate number of briefers	• Number trained • Percentage who pass training exam	• Ten briefers trained • 100 percent pass rate on training exam	
Step 2: Deliver briefing	Briefers	**Process:** Provide briefing at regular intervals **Outcome:** Increase participant awareness about suicide risk factors and hotline	• Number of briefings conducted per month	• Four briefings per month • 50 percent improvement in awareness	
	Soldiers	**Outcome:** Reduce suicide attempts	• Percentage of soldiers who are aware of suicide hotline • Number of documented suicide attempts	• Three fewer documented suicide attempts per year	
Hotline					
Step 1: Train hotline operators	Hotline operators	**Process:** Effectively train an adequate number of operators	• Number trained • Percentage of operators who successfully complete mock hotline calls	• Five operators trained • 100 percent successfully complete mock hotline calls	
Step 2: Answer hotline calls	Hotline operators	**Process:** Answer calls to provide information, referrals, and emergency assistance **Outcome:** Increase completed referrals to mental health care	• Percentage of calls answered within three rings; percentage of emergency calls connected with 911 • Number of referrals made; percentage of completed referrals	• 90 percent of calls answered within three rings; 100 percent of emergency calls connected with 911 • 40-percent increase in completed referrals	
	Soldiers	**Outcome:** Reduce suicide attempts	• Number of documented suicide attempts	• Three fewer documented suicide attempts per year	

How to Select and Populate Performance Measures

For each question that the program performance assessment seeks to answer, it is important to determine which measures to use; this decision should be based on two key characteristics. First, feasibility: How easy or difficult will it be to collect the necessary information on an ongoing basis? For the example above, how will the program determine whether soldiers and their families know about the hotline? Will program staff conduct any focus groups or surveys of soldiers where it will be possible to ask about their awareness of the hotline? For the data on the type and number of calls to the hotline, does the program currently collect this information? How easy or difficult would it be to implement a process to collect these data on a regular basis? Similarly, how is it best to measure whether referrals to mental health care have increased as a result of the hotline? What would it take to follow up on the referrals to assess the degree to which the referrals were completed and the individuals in need received care?

Second, it is important to consider the desired accuracy for these measures. It is helpful to think about whether a rough estimate would serve the assessment's needs or if an exact count is required. Programs often need to balance precision with feasibility; it is often the case that the more precise the data needed, the more difficult they are to collect. In the suicide prevention briefing example, perhaps it is not necessary to know the exact proportion of soldiers and their families who have heard of the hotline; it may be possible to infer through a series of focus groups whether the hotline is well-known or unheard of.

Primary vs. Secondary Data

Data to populate the performance measures can come from a number of sources, which are categorized into primary and secondary data. Primary data refers to new data that the program will collect, while secondary data refers to data that already exist for another purpose. Secondary data could include administrative data, cost information, medical record data, or data from a survey administered for another purpose. These data offer the advantage of already existing, and in some cases, they may include data for all members of a program's target population. However, the data may not be in the optimal format or may not include the needed measures. Secondary data can also be administratively burdensome to acquire or may be costly. Some types of secondary data, such as medical record data, can be much harder to obtain and may be restricted due to privacy concerns.

If secondary data sources will not meet the program's needs or are too difficult to obtain, primary data collection may be necessary. Primary data collection may include surveys with structured questionnaires where respondents can write in answers to the questions, individual interviews, or focus groups. There are many resources to help develop primary data collection efforts (Marczyk, DeMatteo, and Festinger, 2005; Olsen, 2011; Rea and Parker, 2005), and in general, the advantage of this approach is that it supports collecting information on desired measures. However, such data collection can be expensive and time-consuming and must be carefully designed and administered.

Quantitative vs. Qualitative Data

There are several common ways to collect the data for performance measures, and determining the best option depends on what the assessment is measuring. If the assessment is measuring something quantifiable (e.g., number of people who have heard of the program, number of completed referrals), quantitative data for this purpose can be obtained from sources such as responses to survey questions (e.g., yes/no responses or questions that ask survey respondents to select one or more answers from a preset number of options) or administrative data (e.g., costs, counts of participants, or other information that comes from program records).

Qualitative data work best if the assessment seeks to answer a question about perceptions or if not enough is known about the problem. Such nonnumeric information can be obtained by asking open-ended questions of program participants or staff. These sorts of questions can help elicit participant or staff perceptions or beliefs about program activities and performance and identify reasons underlying these perceptions or beliefs. Such questions may also shed light on potential barriers to effective performance. For example, if the assessment sought to understand why soldiers would or would not use the suicide hotline when in distress, it would be best to talk with soldiers to identify barriers or facilitators to use of the hotline. Similarly, if the question asks why hotline staff do not provide referrals to a particular source of care, one approach would be to talk with hotline staff about why and how they determine where to refer soldiers.

Answering many questions about how well a program is working will require both quantitative and qualitative data. If the assessment seeks information about whether the 24-hour suicide prevention hotline has adequate staffing, a first step might be to count the number of calls per hour and the number of calls answered per hour by each hotline operator. An additional step might be to interview a sample of operators to find if they perceive that their workload is too large or if they feel that they could increase the number of calls they are answering.

How to Determine Whether the Program Is Performing as Expected

Once key questions and measures are identified and the requisite data are collected, the data need to be analyzed to determine whether the program is working as expected. We next discuss a general approach to assessing program performance, but note that this is simplified for the purposes of providing an overview. More details are available in Appendix B.

Sampling

If possible, assessing data from all stakeholders in the program is ideal, since this will allow observation of program performance across the entire population of interest. If this is not possible, it is important to select a representative sample of the population from which to collect data. It is important to ensure that the sample is representative—that is, that the sample "looks" like the entire population on important characteristics such as age, gender, rank, marital status, symptom severity, etc.— so that the data can be generalized from the sampled population to the entire population. If the sampled population is not representative, it may lead to incorrect conclusions about program performance. For example, if only individuals with mild symptoms are sampled, and those with more severe symptoms have a different experience of the program, an assessment might come to false conclusions about how well the program is working. As there are a number of ways you might select an appropriate sample, there are many textbooks (Daniel, 2011; Kish, 1965; Lohr, 2010) and additional resources listed in Appendix B that provide more information.

Data Analysis

The best approach to analyzing the data depends on the type of data available. With quantitative data, it is possible to calculate the difference between expected outcomes X and actual outcomes Y. A simple version of this analysis is the following calculation:

$$Expected\ (X) - Actual\ (Y) = Difference\ (Z).$$

The measured difference Z can be used as a measure of how well the program is performing.

Returning to the suicide hotline example, suppose the program could access data obtained from a survey conducted before and after the suicide prevention briefing. Suppose further that the program's goal was to raise awareness about suicide risk factors by 50 percent but that the survey data indicated that, on average, awareness increased by 30 percent. Then the difference Z would equal 20 percent (i.e., 50 percent – 30 percent). This would indicate that the program is having some effect, and a rather large effect, but that the effect is smaller than expected. If, instead, the survey data had indicated that awareness increased by 60 percent, the difference Z would equal –10 percent (i.e., 50 percent – 60 percent), which would indicate that the program is having a bigger effect than expected.

If the performance assessment is using qualitative data from interviews and focus groups, there are a number of ways to understand whether the program is meeting its goals. For example, perhaps the assessment collected data through focus groups with soldiers before and after the suicide prevention briefing and elicited perceptions and beliefs about suicide attempts. While there are numerous resources that describe qualitative analysis (e.g., Bernard and Ryan, 2010; Crabtree and Miller, 1992; Guest and MacQueen, 2008), one way to assess the difference between the "before" and "after" groups is to read through the transcripts or notes from all the focus groups and identify the list of topics (often called themes) that arose spontaneously. For each topic, it should be possible to determine how important it was to the focus group participants. Important topics are often the ones that: (a) are discussed the most, (b) group members are most emphatic about, or (c) seem to generate the most conflict. The next step is to read through these topics and determine to what degree some topics are more likely to arise and seem to be more salient for one set of focus groups compared to the other set. If the "after" focus groups have topics or themes that indicate greater awareness about suicide prevention or less stigma about help-seeking than the "before" groups, it is likely that the briefing is having the intended effect.

Again, we caution that this is a brief overview, intended to provide guidance on assessing actual program performance compared to expected performance. This is not intended to take the place of a formal program evaluation, the methods for which are well described in numerous evaluation textbooks (Patton, 2002; Rossi, Lipsey, and Freeman, 2004). Although it is beyond the scope of this report to describe these methods in detail, additional information and a list of resources are available in Appendix B.

Cautions

There are at least three cautions to keep in mind when assessing how well a program is performing. First, SMART goals are crucial. In particular, it is important to ensure that what the performance assessment is measuring is relevant. Whoever is charged with assessing program performance should not assume that everyone agrees on what a program is supposed to accomplish. A program's objectives and its activities are often implicit rather than explicit and may not be shared by everyone involved. It may be important to come to consensus with relevant stakeholders on the goals and activities of the program before assessing performance. Second, it is important to be precise in stating what the program and its activities are supposed to accomplish when beginning the assessment. Vague goals and objectives are difficult to assess and measure. Third, determining how well the program is working should not be a one-time process but rather should be done on a regular basis. To make the processes easier, it is helpful to consider incorporating mechanisms for collecting and storing assessment information into the program's routine practices.

Identifying Problems in Programs That Are Not Working Well

Chapter Two was designed to help determine whether a program is accomplishing what it was intended to do. Since many programs, despite their best intentions, often fall short of expectations, an important next step is pinpointing where problems are occurring and why. Chapter Three describes this step in detail (Figure 3.1).

Programs underperform or fail across a wide range of activities and for many reasons. It is common for a program to underperform due to multiple problems rather than a single concern. Program managers often find that a few comparatively minor problems can limit a program's effectiveness.

Where Are the Problems Occurring?

To determine what problems are affecting the program, it is helpful to articulate clearly what is supposed to happen in the program. Note that this determination is different from describing program activities, as discussed in Chapter Two. There, the description is intended to be more schematic, addressing the program's stages and activities. Here, it is worth bearing in mind a

Figure 3.1
Overview of Chapter Three

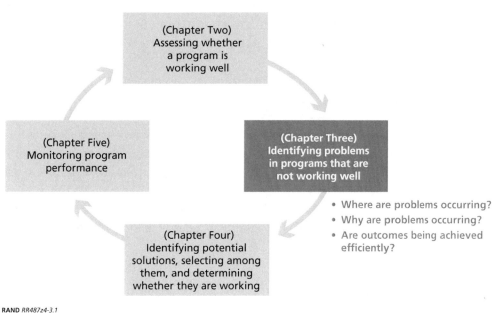

RAND RR487z4-3.1

much more detailed accounting of what is supposed to happen in the program, which staff members are accountable for what activities, how recipients of program services are affected in each activity, and how all of the program's activities are supposed to work when functioning ideally. This activity involves three steps: (a) describing how the program is supposed to work, (b) identifying program staff and their roles in the program, and (c) tracing participants as they move through the program.

Describing How the Program Is Supposed to Work

The first step is to map out how the program ideally is supposed to work. Are there clearly defined steps and processes that lead to the desired outcomes? If so, what are they? Some programs have relatively simple processes. Take the suicide prevention hotline described in Chapter Two. In the simplest case, it is possible to imagine the program to be operationalized as a five-step process:

1. Identify a pool of individuals interested in staffing the hotline but who lack the relevant knowledge and skills.
2. Screen individuals in the pool to determine who should be trained.
3. Provide this group with a training course.
4. Test the individuals to see to what extent participants learned the intended knowledge or skills.
5. Conduct routine assessments of the job performance of the trained individuals.

Note that in some cases, programs may need to rely on the activities of a number of people in different roles to be successful. Take, for instance, the hotline program's responsibility to refer callers for follow-up care. Here, one might imagine a four-step process for those callers who are not in immediate distress:

1. The hotline operator (a) suggests that a caller seek care at a specific referral site (based on a computer algorithm that identifies the site nearest to the caller's home address); (b) offers to make a referral on the caller's behalf; and (c) offers to provide the caller's name, contact information, and a brief description of the situation to the referral site.
2. If the caller agrees, then the hotline operator calls the referral site and provides the caller's information.
3. The referral site contacts the caller and schedules an appointment.
4. The caller attends the appointment.

In this case, it is important to realize that the program's goal of ensuring that individuals receive referral care depends not only on the hotline operator fulfilling his or her duties, but also on the computer program identifying the most appropriate site. In addition, the referral site and the caller must also fulfill their roles.

Describing a program as a sequence of steps will not explain why a program is underperforming, but it will help identify *where* in a program to focus attention in order to improve performance.

Identifying Stakeholders and Their Roles in the Program

Next, for each step, it is important to identify who is involved and what their roles are. This requires distinguishing between those who are responsible for carrying out program activities and those who are intended to receive program services. For this step, it is also important to identify the entities playing a role in the program, such as other organizations, and to remember to include processes or things such as computer software that play a role in providing program services.

Tracing Individuals Through the Program

After describing how the system is supposed to work and which actors are responsible for what, the next step is to look for information about how well the system is functioning at each step. Again, although this is somewhat similar to assessing the performance of the program in Chapter Two, this stage requires much more detail.

The easiest way to do this is to start at the beginning and trace individuals through each step of their interactions with the program. Who engages with the program, and how many people get to the first step? In what time frame? Who successfully gets to the second step, and how many? In what time frame? How many people drop out and disengage from the program? Why, and what are their characteristics? Are there people who get to each of these steps but who are delayed? What else is known about the first step? For instance, were there any exit interviews conducted? If there are no existing data, who could a program manager (or whoever is conducting the assessment) talk to about this step to understand what individuals' experiences are like?

How might this work in our suicide hotline training example? The first step requires identifying a pool of candidates to train in staffing the suicide hotline. At this point it helps to know: (a) how easy it was to identify all the people who belong to the candidate pool, (b) how large this initial pool was, and (c) to what degree the potential pool was likely to include those with the least amount of knowledge about suicide prevention.

In the second step, the program screens all the individuals in the pool to determine who should go for training. Here it is helpful to know: (a) what percentage of the pool was actually screened and how many people were missed (e.g., because they were unavailable when the screening took place), and (b) what number and percentage were found to have the core skills needed to help people in distress and therefore would benefit from training.

In the third step, the program provides the selected individuals with the training course. At this point it is helpful to know: (a) what number and percentage of those designated to receive the training actually received it, (b) for each individual, what kinds of material were they exposed to and how much time they spent in training, (c) how satisfied the participants (instructors and trainees) were with the training, and—most important—(d) how well these individuals did on simulated hotline calls to practice their new skills.

Tracing people through the system allows an evaluator to identify where people are dropping out or where they are not receiving what was expected from the program. This will show where program management may want to concentrate program improvement efforts. In our example, the data might have shown that: (a) the pool of potential participants was appropriately identified; (b) 40 percent of the pool was never screened; (c) of those who were identified as needing additional training, only 50 percent attended the workshops; and (d) of those who attended the workshops, more than 80 percent attended them all, 90 percent were satisfied with what was covered and how the courses were run, and 90 percent performed well enough on simulated calls to begin staffing the hotline. This suggests that improving program performance requires concentrating on steps related to screening, in particular the step that gets those who need training to the actual workshops. It also suggests that program management should spend less effort focusing on how the course is taught, since that part of the program seems to be performing well.

Why Are the Problems Occurring?

Identifying where problems are occurring requires clear information about program operations. Sometimes program managers can use existing information to determine where problems may exist in a program. More often, however, identifying what these problems specifically are and why they occur requires speaking with both the people responsible for running the program and the participants who receive the services of the program at each step.

Eliciting Information from Program Staff

People who are working in a program may only understand those program steps in which they play a role. Although administrators often think they understand each step, they often have second-hand knowledge of what goes on. To clarify what actually works and does not work at any given step, program managers need to get information directly from the program staff involved with that step. Collecting this information may involve some of the techniques used and information gathered in the exploratory data collection. (See Chapter Two for a discussion about ways to collect these types of data.) Below, we provide some examples of types of questions that program managers might want to ask. We continue the example of the suicide prevention program here, focusing on the first step of the hotline: training hotline operators. We note that this process should be repeated for each step of the program.

When speaking to the program staff about training hotline operators, the program manager ideally would ask about all the kinds of things that could possibly go wrong with that step of the program. It is possible to address many of these potential problems by asking nine types of questions to various participants.

1. *What is working and not working in regards to the hotline training?* This is a "grand tour" question because it gives the person being interviewed a chance to give his or her overall assessment of the situation. This kind of free-flowing question is important to ask first as it allows the interviewee to identify the most salient issues.
2. *How well do program staff at this step understand the main objective or goals of the hotline training?* The purpose of this question is to allow a quick assessment of whether the staff have a shared understanding and are working toward the same goals. Significant differences among program staff often suggest that there are different factions or that the expectations are not well-defined or explicit.
3. *How well does everyone understand what specific roles and responsibilities they play in the hotline training?* Answers to this question will reveal whether people are unclear about what they (or others they work with) are supposed to be doing to ensure that the program meets its goals. Often, program operations slow down and lack accountability when people are not sure who is supposed to be doing what specific tasks. For example,

do program staff understand who is supposed to screen potential hotline operators and who is supposed to schedule the training sessions?

4. *How well does everyone understand what counts as good or poor performance on their specific tasks?* Even if staff members are clear about what they or others are supposed to do, participants might be unclear about the standards of performance to which they are held accountable. When standards are not made explicit, it often results in a wide range of performance. Often a few poor performers can have a relatively large negative effect on outcomes.

5. *To what extent are people motivated to carry out their roles and responsibilities?* Incentives are critically important for ensuring that staff perform to the best of their ability. This question is intended to uncover how people are currently positively and negatively motivated for doing their jobs. There are many ways to incentivize people other than monetary rewards, including giving people more control of a particular process, recognizing their work, or instilling a sense of competition for who can do the best work.

6. *What kind of monitoring process (if any) is in place to track staff performance?* Monitoring can be implicit or explicit. An implicit monitoring system might assume that all staff responsible for conducting the hotline training adhere to the training curriculum and that if they were asked about what was covered during the training session after a specific session, the trainer could recall what was covered and in what order the material was presented. A more explicit monitoring system, however, might require the trainer to fill out a paper or computer log, checking a box to indicate that they covered specific elements of the curriculum, noting how many trainees were present during the session, and indicating what the next steps are for the training group. In situations where monitoring is implicit, it is often hard to develop a sense of accountability. If people know they are going to have to fill out an explicit monitoring log, they are far more likely to fulfill all the tasks required.

7. *How is the information from the monitoring process used to identify problems or improve performance?* Highly burdensome monitoring or monitoring for its own sake is usually not a good use of resources, but a monitoring process that is tied to improvement efforts and performance incentives can support strong program performance.

8. *To what degree are people adequately trained to fulfill their roles and responsibilities?* It is relatively easy to assign people roles and responsibilities and to set performance standards. It only takes one or two people who are underperforming to hamper a program's overall performance.

9. *Finally, if the program includes nonhuman entities, such as computer software programs, ask staff who are responsible for operating them, or ask recipients of the outputs from these entities how well they are performing and what might be improved.*

Eliciting Information from Recipients of the Program's Services

Gathering feedback from people who receive the program's services can be critical to informing the assessment of whether the program is meeting its intended objectives. Users often see the programs from the inside and often have unique perspectives on what is going well and what is going poorly. In speaking to program participants (whether individually or in a group), program managers may find it helpful to follow a few relatively simple steps for conducting basic participant interviews or discussion groups.

To do this, it is important to first set the stage so that the program participants providing feedback understand the purpose of the interview or discussion: A program assessment is seeking help in improving the program, and their experiences will provide valuable information. In these conversations, program participants should feel that (a) they are the experts, since they have a unique perspective as users of the program's services; (b) their input is valued and will factor into the program assessment; and (c) they are being asked for a candid, honest assessment—both negative and positive.

The next step is to elicit the participants' overall assessment of the program. For example, the following script could be used in a discussion group with soldiers who attend the briefing on suicide prevention: "Please take a moment and think back about the briefing today from start to finish. Now please tell me about your experience. I really would like to know what you liked and what you didn't like." Note that the last two sentences are: (a) short, (b) ask people to perform a task rather than answer a direct question, and (c) open the possibility for people to respond along the entire positive to negative continuum. These characteristics are important because they help make the request for information and assessment as nonthreatening as possible and are likely to lead to more complete responses.

The objective is to get the person to relay as much information as possible without coaching. Following are a few specific tips to prompt people to talk freely about their experiences:

- Nodding and smiling without saying anything or taking notes can encourage interviewees to volunteer additional information.
- Saying "I see," "that's interesting," or just "Hmm" can show that the interviewer is listening and engaged, again prompting people to say more.
- Repeating back or paraphrasing what the interviewee has just said can prompt an interviewee to elaborate.
- Asking directly, "Can you think of anything else?" or "Please tell me more" can also be helpful.

All of these probes are nonspecific—they do not guide the person to talk about anything in particular. They take advantage of the linguistic phenomenon of "turn-taking." In effect, the interviewer is "skipping a turn" in the conversation by either being silent or saying something that really does not add to the conversation. There are two exceptions to this turn-taking trick: (1) Avoid using the same tactic repeatedly, as the other person may quickly become annoyed; and (2) avoid saying "OK," which usually indicates an end to that conversation and a desire to move on to another topic.

After listening to the overall assessment of the program, the program manager can turn to identifying details at each key step. This requires a clear transition from general to specific. For instance, one approach would be to say, "I know you have already told me a little about this, but I'd like to hear more about your experience—both positive and negative." Now the interviewer can simply repeat the process above for each step of the program that the interviewee can shed light on.

When talking with recipients of program's services it is critical that the interviewer not appear defensive, particularly if interviewees note where a program could be improved.

Finally, it is helpful to make an extra effort to find people who may have dropped out of the program or who had the most negative experiences. In the suicide hotline example, it may be difficult to contact callers who have had a negative experience; however, the program manager should still consider how to do this. For example, perhaps complaints about the hotline have been made; in this case, the program manager could follow up with the individuals who made the complaints to understand specifically what went wrong. Understanding the experiences of these people can provide critical information for program improvement.

Summarizing the Findings

After examining how each step of the program is performing, it is important to summarize where and why the program is underperforming. Often, there are opportunities for improvement at each step in the program process. Ideally, program improvement efforts would address all the issues uncovered in the assessment. In reality, however, the problems addressed will have to be prioritized. It is sometimes useful to list each problem and ask three questions to help set priorities:

1. *How would the program as a whole be affected if improvements addressed a given problem?* The bigger the expected impact, the greater the priority that addressing this problem should be given.

2. *Where is the problem located in the program (i.e., at a step near the beginning, middle, or end of the list of program steps)?* Sometimes it is necessary to fix problems at the beginning of a process before addressing problems toward the end. In the suicide hotline training example above, for instance, assume that the assessment identified two major problems: (a) problems identifying the most appropriate individuals to train as hotline operators and (b) dissatisfaction among individuals who received the training regarding the content and how it was covered. In this case, it makes more sense to address the issue of finding the right individuals to train before dealing with how the training is delivered.

3. *How much effort (in terms of labor, resources, and leadership effort) would it take to address this issue?* This is a counter to the criterion in (1) above. Answering this question requires carefully considering those problems that represent potentially large impacts on the system but that are likely to require considerable resources to address. In contrast, if there are problems that it would take little effort to address, these might be considered higher priorities even if the expected impact of each is small, since multiple small changes can produce large impact.

Cautions

Once again, some cautions are in order for this component of program performance assessment. First, simple and direct answers to the question "What is wrong with this program?" are often oversimplifications and lead to poor assessments of what is really wrong. Go to the best sources of information for each program step—and, whenever possible, get insights from multiple people (staff and recipients of the program's services) who might have different perspectives. Second, be cautious about jumping to conclusions too quickly. For example, some problems that might initially appear to be at the beginning of process may actually be occurring at a later stage. In the suicide hotline example, consider the step of the program where hotline operators make referrals to care for callers in need of help. Assessment of this portion of the program may show that individuals are not getting into care once they are referred by the hotline operator. It might be reasonable to assume that the problem is due to poor follow-though by either the referral site or by the individuals themselves. In fact, the problem may stem from neither. The real issue may be that the referral sites are overburdened because they do not have adequate mechanisms for transitioning some of their clients into other less-intense or longer-term programs. Alternatively, the software program that the hotline operator uses to identify the nearest referral site might be inadequate and need to be modified to identify the nearest site with availability.

Sometimes understanding where the problem is leads to an obvious solution. In other cases, understanding the problem is only the first step. The next step is to develop potential solutions, which is the subject of Chapter Four.

CHAPTER FOUR

Identifying Potential Solutions, Selecting Among Them, and Determining Whether They Are Working

After determining the reason or reasons that a program is not working as well as desired (Chapter Three), the next step is to figure out how to solve the problem, which is the focus of this chapter (Figure 4.1). This involves addressing four questions: (1) How can the program performance assessment identify potential solutions? (2) How can program managers choose among solutions? (3) How can chosen solutions be implemented? (4) How can program managers tell if the chosen solution is working?

There are no simple formulas for deciding where to intervene in a program that is under-performing. You might, however, want to consider some of the following suggestions.

- First, try to address problems for which change will produce the biggest impact for the least amount of effort.

Figure 4.1
Overview of Chapter Four

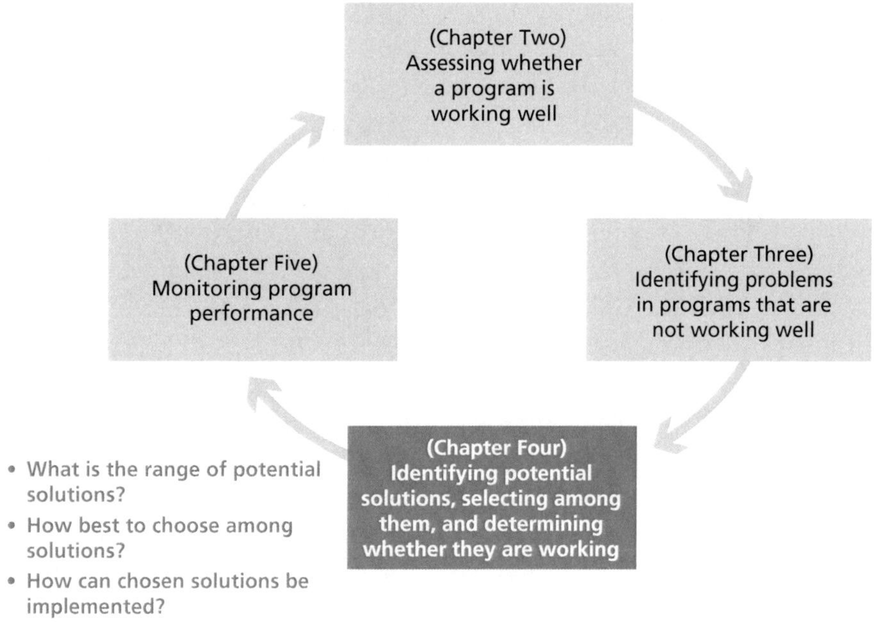

- What is the range of potential solutions?
- How best to choose among solutions?
- How can chosen solutions be implemented?

RAND RR487z4-4.1

23

- Second, pay attention to the details—fixing three or four small problems that require only a small amount of effort may add up to significant impact.
- Third, take a "whole system" approach: Try to envision the system as a series of pipes that have various "leaks" and "clogs." Ask what would happen downstream if improvement efforts targeted a particular leak or clog upstream. For example, plugging a leak at the beginning of a system may have no effect on outcomes because there is a clog later on in the system. In such a case, the program may want to address the clog first and the leak second, or address both problems simultaneously.
- Finally, remember that systems are dynamic; fixing one problem may lead to unintended consequences. For example, a successful intervention to recruit more people into a program may strain capacity in other parts of the program to the point that the program starts to fail in ways it had not before.

How to Identify Potential Solutions

Ideas for potential solutions can come from many different sources. They are found in the professional literature, suggested by people who are interviewed, or derived from common sense and past experiences. The source of the solutions is largely irrelevant—the important thing is to consider as wide and as comprehensive a range of potential solutions as possible, even if they seem unlikely to be implemented when first considered.

One mistake program managers often make is failing to consider the full range of available options and focusing too much attention on one group of people, one process, or one type of program improvement. Service providers frequently lament "If only they (i.e., patients, consumers, end-users) understood how to . . ."—implying that improvements are most likely to come from training or educating the recipient of the services. This is not always true.

Another common mistake is to believe that complex systems can be significantly improved by implementing a single change. Such a belief assumes that most problems are located within a single part of the program and that one fix will address them. This is rarely the case. The most successful quality improvement projects often employ a mix of improvements, often targeting multiple players at different points in the system.

To help ensure that the assessment has not overlooked stakeholders or broad categories of potential solutions, it is helpful to list the program's stakeholders and characterize their perspectives (see Table 4.1). If done as part of a group discussion with members of the program's team or staff, this is likely to generate quite a bit of discussion, as well as a much longer and diverse list of potential solutions than any one individual working alone is likely to produce. To identify the relevant stakeholders, it may be useful to consider a concentric circle, where those who are most involved with the program are at the innermost part of the circle, and those with varying degrees of involvement are in outer circles (see Figure 4.2).

To fill in the grid, begin by identifying a specific problem area to be addressed (i.e., the first line of Table 4.1). If there is more than one problem area, then fill in a separate grid for each one. This information can draw heavily from the descriptive data gathered in the earlier stage of identifying problems. Next, identify the stakeholders who are directly or indirectly involved with this particular problem area. Stakeholder groups include: (a) the different types of staff members who work with the program, (b) other organizations that might assist the program in reaching its goals (e.g., the referral sites described above), and (c) recipients of the

Table 4.1
Grid for Identifying What Is Occurring in Program Problem Areas and Potential Solutions

What is the specific problem to be addressed?

For each group:	Stakeholder Groups			
	Group 1	Group 2	Group 3	Group 4
What are their roles and responsibilities?				
What counts as good and poor performance?				
How are they motivated?				
How is their performance monitored?				
How is the information from the monitoring process used and evaluated?				
How are they trained for their roles?				

program's services. It is important to remember that program management has the most control of the former and the least control of the latter. Write in each stakeholder group in the column headers of Table 4.1.

Finally, fill in the cells of Table 4.1 by trying to answer the following questions as explicitly as possible for each stakeholder group: (1) Were there any problems or issues in regard to each group's roles and responsibilities, and if so, how might these roles and responsibilities be modified to address the issues? (2) Were there any issues in terms of clearly describing what counts as good and poor performance, and if so, how could these standards be modified? (3) Were there any motivational issues identified relative to each of the roles and responsibilities of stakeholders, and if so, what kinds of rewards and punishments might be used to further incentivize the group? (4) Were there any issues related to monitoring group members' performance, and if so, how might the monitoring process be changed? (5) Were there problems with how the information from the monitoring process was used and evaluated to determine rewards and punishments, and if so, how might these processes be improved? (6) Was there any indication that group members were inadequately trained to fulfill their roles and responsi-

Figure 4.2
Identifying Relevant Stakeholders by Level of Involvement with the Program

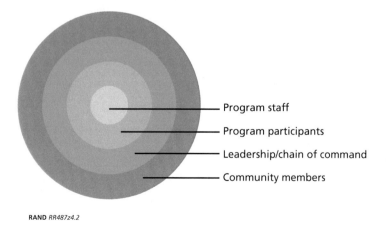

Program staff

Program participants

Leadership/chain of command

Community members

bilities, and if so, what kind of training and education-based interventions might help improve their performance?

Table 4.1a
Suicide Hotline Example

What is the specific problem to be addressed?	Hotline callers needing care are not getting into care once they are referred by the hotline operator		
	Stakeholder Groups		
For each group:	**Group 1** **Hotline callers**	**Group 2** **Hotline operators**	**Group 3** **Referral sites**
What are their roles and responsibilities?	**Ideal:** Follow through on referral	**Ideal:** Provide and coordinate referrals	**Ideal:** Provide care to referred callers
	Current: As specified	**Current:** As specified	**Current:** As specified
		Suggestion: Expand role to follow up with patients who miss first referral visit	**Suggestion:** Expand role to include more proactive follow-up with patients who miss first appointment
What counts as good and poor performance?	**Ideal:** Make first referral visit and stay in care	**Ideal:** Provide appropriate referrals, coordinate with referral site	**Ideal:** Coordinate with hotline operator, accept referrals
	Current: As specified		
		Current: As specified	**Current:** As specified
How are they motivated?	**Ideal:** Self motivated	**Ideal:** Desire to help callers, want to perform well at their job	**Ideal:** Desire to help those in need
	Current: Some do not attend referral visit for multiple reasons	**Current:** Motivated	**Current:** Motivated, but many clinics/providers have too many patients
	Suggestion: Operators use motivational interviewing to encourage callers to make first referral		**Suggestion:** Difficult and beyond call center scope
How is their performance monitored?	**Ideal:** Referral sites contact patients if visit missed	**Ideal:** Self-monitoring; informal feedback from callers and referral sites	**Ideal:** Call center tracks whether callers make their first visit
	Current: Done once	**Current:** Self- and informal monitoring	**Current:** Monitor by call center
	Suggestion: Call center directly follows up with patients who miss first referral visit		
How is the information from the monitoring process used and evaluated?	**Ideal:** Caller responds to contact from referral site	**Ideal:** Call center changes practices to improve quality	N/A
	Current: Not sufficient	**Current:** As specified	
	Suggestion: Call center does follow-up and helps remove barriers to care		
How are they trained for their roles?	**Ideal:** Education provided by call center focuses on providing information about referral sites	**Ideal:** Training focused on linking callers to care	N/A
		Current: As specified	
	Current: As specified	**Suggestion:** Provide motivational interview training to encourage first referral visit	

Below is an example of how this grid might be completed using the suicide prevention program example we have been discussing throughout this report. For this grid, the specific problem to be addressed is that a significant number of hotline callers needing care are not getting into care once they are referred by the hotline operator. The key stakeholders involved during the referral and follow-up stages are: (a) the hotline callers, (b) the hotline operators, and (c) the referral sites. These go in the columns of Table 4.1a. After interviewing a sample of hotline operators, the program evaluator discovers that for the most part, hotline operators are doing their jobs—including setting up appointments with appropriate referral sites, making sure that hotline callers know where to go as well as the day and time of their appointment, and contacting referral sites to monitor how many callers got to their initial visit. Referral sites report being ready to receive hotline callers, leaving reminder messages for hotline callers the day before their appointment and trying to contact those who miss their appointments to see if they want to reschedule. Hotline callers who made their appointments appeared more or less satisfied with the care they received. Hotline callers who did not receive care, however, for the most part recognized the importance of getting care, but report missing their initial appointments for a wide range of reasons including (but not limited to) feeling severely depressed, worrying about being stigmatized, being unable to take time off from work, and lacking the transportation to get there. The results of these interviews are recorded under the subheadings "Ideal" and "Current" in the cells of Table 4.1a.

After completing the grid for each stakeholder group, a program evaluator can use the results to think about which groups to target for particular types of program improvements. The grid forces the program improvement team to consider the different types of people and nonhuman entities, such as computer software programs, that can be the targets of steps to improve program performance and the broad range of actions that may lead to improvements—including changing expectations, redefining roles and responsibilities, improving motivation, establishing more effective monitoring and evaluation processes, and building capacity. This information can then help create a list of potential solutions.

In the suicide prevention example, the evaluator heard a variety of suggestions on how to improve the situation. Three of the most prominent included: (1) having hotline operators use motivational interviewing techniques with all callers to get them to their first referral appointment; (2) asking referral sites to be more proactive in following up with callers who do not make their appointments; (3) having the call center take more responsibility for following up with patients who do not make their appointments, including trying to eliminate barriers that are preventing them from getting into care. These suggestions have been incorporated into Table 4.1a.

Choosing Among Solutions

Now that a list of potential solutions exists, the next step is to assess the pros and cons of each. The objective of this step is not to identify the "best" solution, since no solution addresses every problem; rather, the objective is to make explicit the trade-offs among solutions.

Table 4.2 presents a guide for weighing potential solutions and choosing among them. To fill in this grid, the first step is determining which criteria are most important for selecting among the list of previously identified solutions. Criteria can often be articulated in the form of a question. For example, how effective is the solution likely to be? How much will it cost in

Table 4.2
Guide for Selecting Among Potential Solutions

Potential Solutions	Selection Criteria				
	Criterion 1	Criterion 2	Criterion 3	Criterion 4	Criterion 5
Solution A					
Solution B					
Solution C					
Solution D					

terms of money and resources? What kinds of additional burdens might the solution place on participants? How long will it take to implement? To what degree is it logistically feasible? How politically realistic is it? How might the solution be limited by other policies or regulations? How are those most affected by the changes likely to react? How might others be affected? Each key criterion should be listed as a separate column in the grid and each potential solution should be represented as a separate row.

Once the rows and columns have been identified, the next step is to fill in each of the cells. At this point, it is necessary to determine what types of data are required for each column and what level of detail is required for the data. Some of the columns are likely to require some sort of relative scale. The level of precision needed, however, may vary from one criterion to another. For instance, in estimating the cost of a solution, an actual dollar amount (e.g., $10,000) might be useful, or a simpler ranking that organizes costs along a relative scale of high/medium/low might be sufficient. Other columns may require text descriptions rather than scales. For example, answering the question, "How might others be affected?" may require consideration of both the pros and the cons of the potential solution.

Once the grid has been completed, the final step is to order the list of potential solutions from most to least favorable. One way to begin is to identify those potential solutions that are clear winners and losers based on the criteria. In practice, some of the potential solutions can often be eliminated fairly quickly. Solutions that are overly expensive, logistically unfeasible, or violate preexisting policies or regulations can often be rejected. In contrast, winners are those solutions that appear to be effective, are relatively inexpensive, easy to implement, politically feasible, and otherwise seem to have few downsides. Such solutions are usually quite rare, and most potential solutions fall somewhere in between these two extremes. Effective solutions are often costly, take additional efforts to implement, and may not be universally endorsed by all those involved, while solutions that are less expensive, more acceptable, and easy to implement logistically are often less effective at resolving the challenges that programs face.

There is no exact science to selecting among alternative solutions, and the grid in Table 4.2 is not designed to provide a means of calculating a simple answer. Instead, the grid is designed to make key selection criteria explicit, assess each potential solution in terms of these key criteria, and act as a guide for discussions about these issues. Team members and other stakeholders are essential partners in this process, and the importance of actively engaging them in weighing potential solutions cannot be overemphasized.

It is sometimes helpful to divide the final selection process into stages. Once the grid is complete, have a discussion as a team about the pros and cons of the various solutions. The objective here is to identify the two or three most promising solutions or packages of solutions.

After identifying a more limited set, these options can be presented to the different groups that are most likely to be affected by any changes that might implemented. Specifically ask representatives of each group what they see as the pros and cons of each potential solution, what key issues will need to be addressed, and what their recommendations are for ensuring that the solutions have the greatest impact and fewest problems during implementation. Meetings with various groups of stakeholders not only generate more information about each solution and how it might be implemented, but also help gain buy-in from those groups that are most likely to be affected by these decisions.

Table 4.2a shows how the grid above might be used to evaluate the three potential solutions in the suicide prevention example. Each row represents one of the three solutions identified in the previous step, and the columns represent four key criteria for evaluating the solutions. The first criterion refers to the amount of control that the suicide prevention program has over making changes to the current system. The second examines the amount of additional work that call operators and other staff will have to shoulder. The third considers what other changes will be required, such as hiring additional personnel or developing data systems. The final criterion estimates the potential impact of each of the solutions.

In this example, suppose that determining criteria to use and what values to put in each cell came as a result of a team discussion. For instance, the team felt it was important to recognize that the suicide prevention program would be the primary initiator of any solution. Therefore, they had control of how solutions would be implemented within their program but had relatively little control over how such solutions would be implemented in referral sites or other institutions. In assessing the three solutions along this particular dimension, they determined that they had most control over training their own hotline operators in motivational interviewing techniques and the least control over getting other referral sites to be more active in following up with callers who missed their first appointment. Once the grid was completed, the team could use the grid to have a more thorough and explicit discussion of the pros and cons of each solution. In this case, they concluded that they would try implementing Solution 1 in the short term and move toward Solution 3 over time. Although they realized that the impact of Solution 1 was unlikely to be high, they felt that they had control over the process, it required relatively little investment in staff time and other changes, and it could be imple-

Table 4.2a
Suicide Hotline Example

Potential Solutions	Selection Criteria				
	Amount of Control	Burden for Hotline Staff	Other changes required	Time Frame	Estimated Impact
1. Train hotline operators in motivational interviewing techniques	High	Operators: Medium Other: Low	Hire trainer for motivational interviewing	Short	Low to Medium
2. Get referral sites to be more active in following up with callers who miss their first appointments	Low	Operators: Low Other: High	Staff member needed to work closely with referral sites	Medium to Long	Low
3. Have the call center follow up with patients who miss their first appointment and help eliminate barriers to getting care	Medium to High	Operators: Medium Other: Medium	Develop system to identify missed visits, contact soldiers, and respond to needs	Long	High

mented quickly. They also recognized that in the long run, they would need to make more significant investments in terms of developing systems for tracking callers and working with them to eliminate a wide range of barriers that kept them from getting appropriate care.

Determining Whether the Chosen Solution Works

In an ideal world, program management would pilot-test the changes using a structured approach designed to accurately tell whether the changes are causing the desired effect. A rigorous design would compare two groups: (1) participants in the program with the added changes and (2) participants in the program without the added changes. There are several ways to do this, including a small randomized controlled trial (RCT). Although it is beyond the scope of this report to describe these methods in detail, additional information and a list of resources are available in Appendix B.

Since many programs may have limited available time or resources, the most practical method for evaluating whether the solution identified actually fixes the problems and improves program performance is to follow an approach that is often known as "Plan—Do—Study—Act" (Langley et al., 2009; Deming, 2000). This approach could also be known as "try it and see if it works," though it is important to point out that it is not quite as easy as it sounds, since doing so requires determining how exactly to measure whether the changes are working before considering any further changes.

The first step is to *plan* how to test the solution. It is important to be specific here, and to identify what the goal is, what is expected to happen as a result of implementing the solution, and what kind of data the assessment needs to collect. This is very similar to the steps in Chapter Two, but on a smaller scale and focusing only on the proposed change.

Chapter Two identified a number of measures for assessing program performance. Depending on the nature of the problem identified and what the goal of the solution is, the measures for evaluating the effect of the solution may or may not be the same. For example, suppose the initial assessment of program performance found that few people were completing referrals. Then, suppose that one of the problems identified was that the computer system used to generate local resources for referrals did not generate good matches (e.g., referral sources were located far from the caller, or did not provide the needed type of care or service). In this case, it might still be desirable to know the rate of completed referrals, but it may also be important to measure the accuracy of the suggested referrals for each caller. The key is to identify measures that will help determine (1) whether the solution is resolving the specific problem identified, and (2) whether solving the identified problem improves program performance.

During this planning step, it is also important to be realistic about the speed of the expected change. How quickly is change likely to occur and what will the rate of change look like? For example, do you expect to see most of the change occur in the first few months or is change likely to start out slowly and increase over a much longer time period? The more explicit you can be in the planning stage the better.

The second step is to *do* it. Implement the solution on a small scale and collect the necessary data. Perhaps implementation happens for a small number of program participants or program staff, at only one site, or for a limited amount of time. The reason for testing out the solution on a small scale first is to preserve resources; making changes to a program can be costly and time-consuming. It is important to be sure that the changes will have the desired effect in solving the problem before implementing them across the entire program.

The third step is to *study* whether the solution had the desired effect. This may require some analysis of the data. Refer to Chapter Two for a description of how to conduct this analysis.

The final step is to *act*: make changes to the solution, try a different solution (in the case where the solution did not have the hoped-for effect) or implement the solution throughout the program if it was successful.

Implementing the Solution Across the Program

After choosing a solution or set of solutions and testing their effectiveness, program management needs to implement them across the program. Implementation typically involves multiple steps, such as informing people about the changes that are coming, ensuring that they understand why the changes are necessary, and verifying that those in their chain of command are aware of the implementation plan. A step-by-step implementation strategy can help managers anticipate and plan for these types of effects, decide exactly how to implement a given change to the program, clarify who will be responsible for each step, and develop an implementation timeline.

In addition, implementing most changes means that at least some people will need to change how they think and what they do. More often than not, changes ripple outward to affect more people than originally intended. Assume, for instance, that the operators of our example suicide hotline need to perform an additional task beyond what they are currently doing. It would not be surprising to find that to accommodate the new task, hotline operators reduce their efforts in other areas of their job (intentionally or unintentionally) and the reduction in the hotline operators' effort results in other people needing to compensate or in a lowering of the program's overall quality and effectiveness.

Implementing changes often takes longer than expected. Building in time to assess progress in the middle of the change process is often helpful. If program improvements are already behind schedule, extra time can be used to catch up or to reevaluate some of the next steps so that some tasks might be eliminated or their timeline could be shortened.

Finally, the process of implementation is filled with uncertainty. It is unreasonable to expect to anticipate all the issues that will arise during program improvement activities. Since many issues will need to be addressed and resolved as improvement activities occur, it is often useful for program staff to be involved in how these decisions are made.

Cautions

Too often, potentially good solutions fail because of poor implementation. Implementation is a complex process of people performing tasks and making decisions over time. As with any other complex operation, it is essential to ensure that the appropriate order for various tasks has been established, that individual responsibilities are clear, and that individuals have the time and resources needed to effectively implement what they are responsible for.

CHAPTER FIVE

Next Steps and Conclusions

Assessing program performance is a critical task for any program. In a context of limited funding and resources, programs must be able to show that they are meeting established goals and are working as well as possible. By carefully spelling out SMART goals and establishing mechanisms for identifying and resolving threats to program performance, program managers and other stakeholders can be confident that programs are meeting mission needs. The task for programs is to implement a system of CQI by completing the steps outlined in Chapters Three and Four to identify and resolve any staff or system problems that may be impeding performance. This chapter addresses the final step in any program assessment and improvement process: developing a system for ongoing monitoring of program performance.

Ongoing Monitoring of Program Performance

Once the program is working well, it is vital to maintain its performance. A program's effectiveness and efficiency tend to diminish over time for many reasons. Sometimes a change in key personnel, a new policy or regulation imposed from outside the program, or a reduction in budget or manpower can affect program performance. To ensure that any problems are identified early on, it is important to establish a mechanism for ongoing monitoring of program performance.

To do this, it is helpful to determine what outcomes are most important and how to monitor them (see Chapter Two). The next requirement is developing a mechanism to periodically assess the data to determine whether the outcomes are moving in the right direction.

Establishing Data Collection and Monitoring Systems

Ongoing monitoring requires establishing a regular mechanism for collecting and analyzing these data.

In developing a data collection mechanism, it will be important to consider a number of questions:

1. How often will the program collect data? If surveys are used, how often will program staff field the survey? For administrative data, can these be collected continuously?
2. How frequently will program staff analyze the data and assess program performance?
3. How and where will the program store the data?
4. Are there adequate resources (staff, analytic capacity, data storage) for ongoing monitoring?

5. Who will be responsible for monitoring performance of the program as well as the actors responsible for carrying out the program?

Continuous Quality Improvement

Throughout this report we have described the mechanics of carrying out the initial steps of a process of CQI as applied to program performance assessment. Once program managers have articulated the program's goals and measures, established mechanisms to collect and assess information about the program, reviewed the data, decided how the program might be improved, and implemented the changes, the latter steps of the process must begin anew. Then, program management waits until the next cycle of data becomes available and examines how well the implemented changes improved program performance measures. Regardless of whether improvements occur, the new data must be examined to determine next steps in further modifying the program. Repeating the process of collecting, evaluating information, and modifying the program based on this information forms the core of a strong CQI effort. There is one caution to note about the CQI process: It is often tempting to make changes to the program with each cycle of performance data, regardless of how small a change in performance has been observed. It is often better to wait, collect more data (i.e., perhaps several months' worth) to determine if the observed decreased performance is a trend, in which case making changes to the program likely makes sense.

Conclusions

Programs and the policy context in which they operate change frequently. It is important to regularly assess whether the stated goals of the program are meeting an identified need in the target population, and whether there is continued financial and political support for program activities.

High-quality programs can be challenging to maintain and require constant monitoring. Small modifications to programs may be needed on a routine basis to adapt to the ever-changing circumstances in which they operate.

Ensuring that a program is performing as efficiently as possible requires ongoing effort. If strong mechanisms for measuring the program's processes and outcomes are established (see Chapter Two), then this task becomes relatively easy. With periodic checks and ongoing monitoring, program management can identify early warning signs that the program may be going off course. If the program begins to show signs of underperforming, then it can be helpful to identify where the program is having troubles (see Chapter Three) and what kinds of modifications to consider, along with the advantages and disadvantages of each (see Chapter Four).

All programs have challenges, underperform in unexpected ways, or have unintended consequences. Many of these problems can be fixed to help programs operate more effectively and efficiently, using the processes described in this report in an iterative way to ensure that as many problems are addressed as possible.

Program Worksheet for Assessing Performance

Complete the following grid, using one row per program activity or process.

Activity or Process	Target Population	Outcome/Process	Goal	Measure

Guiding questions for each component of the matrix:

Activity or process

1. What are the core features of the program? What does the program do?
2. What interventions or actions does the program perform?
3. How does the program interact with participants?

Target population

1. Does the program serve only one population, or many? Describe the population served.
2. At whom are the program's activities targeted?

Outcomes

Outcomes are those changes or benefits resulting from program activities. Programs typically have short-, intermediate-, and long-term outcomes (Leviton et al., 2010; Wholey, Hatry, and Newcomer, 2010).

1. What changes are expected as a result of the program?
2. Compared to people who are not enrolled in the program, how will participants be different after having experienced the program?
3. What are the anticipated short- and long-term effects of the program on its participants?

Processes

Processes are the "nuts and bolts" of how a program works.

1. What are the steps of the program? For this piece, it may be helpful to draw out a flow diagram as described in Chapter Two.

2. If the program has a user guide or an implementation guide, consider the different components of the program as outlined in the document.
3. Who are the key players (e.g., trainers, coaches, case managers) and what do they do?

Goals

In identifying and specifying goals, it is important to be as explicit as possible, using real numbers or measureable effects.

1. What is the estimated impact or explicit goal for each process or outcome?
2. Are there political or command directives detailing the expected goal (e.g., 100 percent of a group of service members receive suicide prevention training)?
3. Have there been any studies or evaluations of the program, or pieces of the program, in the past? What have these found with respect to the effect of the program? Quantify this effect and be as explicit as possible (e.g., reduce documented suicide attempts by 20 percent).
4. Have there been studies or evaluations of similar programs? What have these found?

Measures

A process is needed to determine how to measure each process or outcome so that actual values can be compared against the specified goal.

1. Consider data availability and feasibility. Is there a way to measure the process or outcome using data that are already being collected?
2. Consider precision: Is an exact number needed or is a rough estimate good enough?

Formal Program Evaluation

There are numerous resources that describe rigorous methods for determining the effect of a change in program activities on outcomes, and more generally on how to complete a formal program evaluation. A number of these resources are listed at the end of this appendix, although it should be noted that this list is by no means complete.

Briefly, there are a number of methodologies for determining the effect of changes to the program (e.g., solutions to problems) on program performance by comparing (1) participants in the program WITH the added changes and (2) participants in the program WITHOUT the added changes (or, for a formal evaluation, comparing individuals who have participated in the program with those who have not).

- **RCT.** This is considered the "gold standard" of research designs. In an RCT, individuals are randomly assigned to either an intervention group (in this case, the program with the added changes) or a control group (the program without the changes). Since individuals are randomly assigned, the two groups will be very similar in terms of numbers of men and women, average age, and other characteristics. This is important because it would mean that any difference observed in outcomes between the two groups is likely due to the intervention (the changes made to the program) rather than other factors.

- **Pre-post design.** This is a very common design, where individuals are compared to themselves at two time points: before and after the intervention. In this case, data are collected on the outcomes of interest from participants in the program before making any changes. Then, the changes are implemented and data are collected on the same outcomes from the same individuals after some time has passed. Although there may be some fallacies in determining that any observed differences between the time points are due to the implemented changes (e.g., the outcomes might have changed on their own anyway), this design can be useful.

- **Time series.** This design is a variation on the pre-post design. Instead of collecting data on the population once before and once after implementing changes to the program, data are collected over time. For example, the data may be collected monthly for the three to six months before implementing the changes, and then for the three to six months following the changes. The strength of this design is that it allows detection of whether there are trends in the outcomes examined (i.e., whether there is a trend toward improving or worsening outcomes) and, if so, whether making the changes affects the direction or slope of the trend.

Choosing which of these designs to use is usually a matter of practicality. The ability to implement ideal designs is often constrained, as programs may lack the resources or time to conduct the most rigorous assessment. In considering the options, programs may want to consider the following questions.

1. **What are the most significant anticipated challenges in determining the effect of the changes on program performance?** There are many things that can mask the real effect an intervention is having on the outcomes measured, known as *threats to validity*. It is important to consider which threats are most probable or most concerning for any given situation. First, as mentioned above, outcomes can change over time without any intervention. Think of a program that is providing group support to individuals with posttraumatic stress disorder. People who participate in the group may have their symptoms increase or decrease over time for reasons having nothing to do with the program—maybe they started taking a new medication, or have experienced a new traumatic event. Table B.1 shows some common threats to validity and the design solutions that best account for these.

2. **What resources are available?** This is not necessarily about money. In evaluating the effect of implemented changes, it is important to consider the capacity of available personnel. Do staff have the time to collect data and the knowledge to use the data to estimate the effect of the changes on program performance? Does the program have the technical ability to collect and analyze data (computers, software programs)?

3. **How much time is available?** While pilot testing the planned changes to the program is the best way to determine whether they will have the desired effect, doing this takes time. Depending on the nature of the program and the types of changes being made, a structured approach could take anywhere from a month to a year. The quickest of the designs mentioned above is the pre-post design, since this only requires data collection at two time points and does not require collecting data from a randomized comparison group. In some cases, the time it takes to pilot test changes to a program is acceptable, since the changes are cumbersome or costly, and it is important to carefully implement and evaluate them. In other cases, the program may be under pressure to adapt and disseminate as quickly as possible.

Table B.1
Some Common Threats to Validity

Threat to Validity	Posttraumatic Stress Disorder Support Group Example	Design Solution
Confounding: changes in outcomes may be attributable to something other than the intervention	Posttraumatic stress disorder symptoms improve because of medication, rather than the support group	RCT; Time series
Selection: individuals receiving the intervention differ in significant ways from those not receiving the intervention	Members of the posttraumatic stress disorder support group have more severe symptoms than those not in the support group	RCT
Diffusion: individuals in the comparison group end up receiving the intervention	Command determines that everyone with posttraumatic stress disorder should be in a support group	Time series; pre-post

Published Resources

Andersen R. "Methods And Problems In Evaluation Of Primary Health Care: Does It Matter Which Way We Go?" Paper presented at: Conference on Evaluation of Primary Health Care; October 28–29, 1991; Center for Primary Care Research, University of Uppsala, Uppsala Sweden.

Brindis C, Hughes DC, Halfon N, Newacheck PW. "The Use of Formative Evaluation to Assess Integrated Services for Children." *Evaluation and The Health Professions*, 1998, 21 (1): 66–90.

Centers for Disease Control and Prevention. Office of the Director, Office of Strategy and Innovation. *Introduction to Program Evaluation for Public Health Programs: A Self-Study Guide.* Atlanta: Centers for Disease Control and Prevention, 2005.

Chinman M, Imm P, Wandersman A. *Getting to Outcomes™ 2004: Promoting Accountability Through Methods and Tools for Planning, Implementation, and Evaluation.* Santa Monica, CA: RAND Corporation, TR-101-CDC. As of April 16, 2013: http://www.rand.org/pubs/technical_reports/TR101.html

Creswell, JW. *Research Design: Qualitative, Quantitative, and Mixed Methods Approaches.* Thousand Oaks, CA: SAGE Publications, 2008.

de Vries H, Weijts W, Dijkstra M, Kok G. "The Utilization of Qualitative and Quantitative Data for Health Education Program Planning, Implementation, and Evaluation: A Spiral Approach." *Health Education Quarterly*, 1992, 19 (1): 101–115.

Donabedian A. "Promoting Quality Through Evaluating the Process of Patient Care." *Medical Care*, 1968, 6 (3): 181–202.

Donaldson SI, Scriven M. *Evaluating Social Programs and Problems: Visions for the New Millennium.* Mahwah, NJ: Erlbaum, 2003.

Glasgow RE, Vogt TM, Boles SM. "Evaluating the Public Health Impact of Health Promotion Interventions: The RE-AIM Framework." *American Journal of Public Health*, 1999, 89 (9): 1322–1327.

Green LW, Kreuter MW. *Health Program Planning: An Educational and Ecological Approach.* Boston: McGraw-Hill, 2005.

Hatry HP. "Sorting the Relationships Among Performance Measurement, Program Evaluation, and Performance Management." *New Directions for Evaluation*, 2013, 2013 (137): 19–32.

Henry GT, Mark, MM. "Beyond Use: Understanding Evaluation's Influence on Attitudes and Actions." *American Journal of Evaluation*, 2003, 24 (3): 293.

Israel BA, Cummings KM, Dignan MB, Heaney CA, et al. "Evaluation of Health Education Programs: Current Assessment and Future Directions." *Health Education Quarterly*, 1995, 22 (3): 364–389.

Jadad AR, Enkin MW. *Randomized Controlled Trials: Questions, Answers and Musings.* Oxford: Blackwell Publishing, 2008.

Katz MH. *Evaluating Clinical and Public Health Interventions: A Practical Guide to Study Design and Statistics.* New York: Cambridge University Press, 2010.

Lincoln YS, Guba EG. *Naturalistic Inquiry*, Vol. 75. Thousand Oaks, CA: SAGE Publications, 1985.

Litwin MS. *How to Measure Survey Reliability and Validity.* Thousand Oaks, CA: SAGE Publications, 1995.

Marczyk GR, DeMatteo D, Festinger, D. *Essentials of Research Design and Methodology.* New York: John Wiley & Sons, 2005.

McDavid JC, Hawthorn LR. *Program Evaluation and Performance Measurement: An Introduction to Practice.* Thousand Oaks, CA: SAGE Publications, 2006.

Nielsen SB, Hunter DEK. "Special Issue: Performance Management and Evaluation," *New Directions for Evaluation*, 2013, 2013 (137): 1–123.

Nezu AM, Nezu CM. *Evidence-Based Outcome Research: A Practical Guide to Conducting Randomized Controlled Trials for Psychosocial Interventions.* New York: Oxford University Press, 2008.

Patton MQ. *Qualitative Research and Evaluation Methods*, 3rd Edition. Thousand Oaks, CA: SAGE Publications, 2002.

Rea LM, Parker RA. *Designing and Conducting Survey Research: A Comprehensive Guide.* San Francisco: Jossey-Bass, 2012.

Rossi PH, Lipsey MW, Freeman HE. *Evaluation: A Systematic Approach.* Thousand Oaks, CA: SAGE Publications, 2004.

Scriven M. *Evaluation Thesaurus.* Thousand Oaks, CA: SAGE Publications, 1991.

Tashakkori A, Teddlie C. *Mixed Methodology: Combining Qualitative and Quantitative Approaches*, Vol. 46. Thousand Oaks, CA: SAGE Publications, 1998.

Vogt WP, Johnson RB. *Dictionary of Statistics and Methodology: A Nontechnical Guide for the Social Sciences.* Thousand Oaks, CA: SAGE Publications, 2011.

Wholey JS, Hatry HP, Newcomer KE (eds.). *Handbook of Practical Program Evaluation*, Vol. 19. San Francisco: Jossey-Bass, 2010.

Yin RK, Bateman PG, Moore GB. "Case Studies and Organizational Innovation Strengthening the Connection." *Science Communication*, 1985, 6 (3): 249–260.

References

Acosta J, Gonzalez GC, Gillen EM, Garnett J, Farmer CM, Weinick RM. *The Development and Application of the RAND Program Classification Tool: The RAND Toolkit, Volume 1.* Santa Monica, CA: RAND Corporation, RR-487/1-OSD, 2014. As of January 2014:
http://www.rand.org/pubs/research_reports/RR487z1.html

Bernard HR, Ryan GW. *Analyzing Qualitative Data: Systematic Approaches.* Thousand Oaks, CA: SAGE Publications, 2010.

Berwick DM, Godfrey AB, Roessner J. *Curing Health Care: New Strategies for Quality Improvement.* San Francisco, CA: John Wiley & Sons, Inc., 1990.

Centers for Disease Control and Prevention. "Writing SMART Objectives: Evaluation Brief No. 3b." 2009. As of July 10, 2013:
http://www.cdc.gov/healthyyouth/evaluation/pdf/brief3b.pdf

Chowanec GD. "Continuous Quality Improvement: Conceptual Foundations and Application to Mental Health Care." *Hospital and Community Psychiatry*, Vol. 45, No. 8, 1994, 789–793.

Crabtree BF, Miller WL. "A Template Approach to Text Analysis: Developing and Using Codebooks," in *Doing Qualitative Research.* BF Crabtree and WL Miller (eds.). Thousand Oaks, CA: SAGE Publications, 1992, 93–109.

Daniel J. *Sampling Essentials: Practical Guidelines for Making Sampling Choices.* Thousand Oaks, CA: SAGE Publications, 2011.

DCoE—*See* Defense Centers of Excellence for Psychological Health and Traumatic Brain Injury.

Defense Centers of Excellence for Psychological Health and Traumatic Brain Injury. "Program Evaluation Guide." 2012. As of March 27, 2013:
http://www.dcoe.health.mil/Content/Navigation/Documents/DCoE_Program_Evaluation_Guide.pdf

Deming WE. *Out of the Crisis.* Cambridge, MA: Massachusetts Institute of Technology, Center for Advanced Engineering Study, 1986.

Deming WE. *The New Economics for Industry, Government, Education*, 2nd ed. Cambridge, MA: The MIT Press, 2000.

Doran GT. "There's a S.M.A.R.T. Way to Write Management's Goals and Objectives." *Management Review*, Vol. 70, No. 11, 1981, 35–36.

Guest G, MacQueen KM. *Handbook for Team-Based Qualitative Research.* Walnut Creek, CA: AltaMira Press, 2008.

Kish L. *Survey Sampling.* Oxford, England: Wiley, 1965.

Langley GL, Moen RD, Nolan KM, Nolan TW, Norman CL, Provost LP. *The Improvement Guide: A Practical Approach to Enhancing Organizational Performance*, 2nd ed. San Francisco, CA: Jossey-Bass, 2009.

Leebov W, Ersoz CJ. *The Health Care Manager's Guide to Continuous Quality Improvement.* Lincoln, NE: Authors Choice Press, 2003.

Leviton LC, Khan LK, Rog D, Dawkins N, Cotton D. "Evaluability Assessment to Improve Public Health Policies, Programs, and Practices." *Annual Review of Public Health*, Vol. 31, 2010, 213–233.

Lohr SL. *Sampling: Design and Analysis*, 2nd ed. Boston, MA: Cengage Learning, 2010.

Marczyk G, DeMatteo D, Festinger D. *Essentials of Research Design and Methodology*. Hoboken, NJ: John Wiley & Sons, Inc., 2005.

Martin LT, Farris C, Adamson DM, Weinick RM. *A Systematic Process to Facilitate Evidence-Informed Decisionmaking Regarding Program Expansion: The RAND Toolkit, Volume 3*, Santa Monica, CA: RAND Corporation, RR-487/3-OSD, 2014. As of January 2014:
http://www.rand.org/pubs/research_reports/RR487z3.html

Olsen W. *Data Collection: Key Debates and Methods in Social Research*. London: SAGE Publications Ltd., 2011.

Patton MQ. *Qualitative Research and Evaluation Methods*, 3rd ed. Thousand Oaks, CA: SAGE Publications, 2002.

Rea LM, Parker RA. *Designing and Conducting Survey Research: A Comprehensive Guide*, 3rd ed. San Francisco, CA: John Wiley & Sons, Inc., 2005.

Rossi PH, Lipsey MW, and Freeman HE. *Evaluation: A Systematic Approach*, 7th ed. Thousand Oaks, CA: SAGE Publications, 2004.

Shortell SM, O'Brien JL, Carman JM, Foster RW, Hughes EFX, Boerstler H, O'Connor EJ. "Assessing the Impact of Continuous Quality Improvement/Total Quality Management: Concept versus Implementation." *HSR: Health Services Research*, Vol. 30, No. 2, 1995, 377–401.

Solberg, LI, Fischer LR, Wei F, Rush WA, Conboy KS, Davis TF, Heinrich RL. "A CQI Intervention to Change the Care of Depression: A Controlled Study." *Effective Clinical Practice*, Vol. 4, No. 6, 2001, 239–249. As of July 10, 2013:
http://www.acponline.org/clinical_information/journals_publications/ecp/novdec01/solberg.htm

Tanielian T, Jaycox LH (eds.). *Invisible Wounds of War: Psychological and Cognitive Injuries, Their Consequences, and Services to Assist Recovery*. Santa Monica, CA: RAND Corporation, MG-720-CCF, 2008. As of October 8, 2013:
http://www.rand.org/pubs/monographs/MG720.html

Weinick RM, Beckjord EB, Farmer CM, Martin LT, Gillen EM, Acosta J, Fisher MP, Garnett J, Gonzalez GC, Helmus TC, Jaycox LH, Reynolds K, Salcedo N, Scharf DM. *Programs Addressing Psychological Health and Traumatic Brain Injury Among U.S. Military Servicemembers and Their Families*. Santa Monica, CA: RAND Corporation, TR-950-OSD, 2011. As of October 8, 2013:
http://www.rand.org/pubs/technical_reports/TR950.html

Wholey JS, Hatry HP, Newcomer KE, *Handbook of Practical Program Evaluations*. San Francisco, CA: John Wiley & Sons, Inc., 2010.